| DATE DUE | | | |
|---|---|---|---|
|  |  |  |  |
|  |  |  |  |
|  |  |  |  |
|  |  |  |  |
|  |  |  |  |
|  |  |  |  |
|  |  |  |  |
|  |  |  |  |
|  |  |  |  |
|  |  |  |  |
|  |  |  |  |
|  |  |  |  |
|  |  |  |  |

# WORLD ABOUT US

# TOXIC WASTE

**M. SPENCE**

GLOUCESTER PRESS
New York·London·Toronto·Sydney

© Aladdin Books Ltd 1992

First published in
the United States in 1992 by
Gloucester Press Inc.
95 Madison Avenue
New York, NY 10016

Design: David West
Children's
Book Design
Designer: John Kelly
Editor: Fiona Robertson
Illustrator: Simon Bishop
Consultant: Madeleine Cobbing,
Greenpeace

Spence, Margaret.
Toxic waste / by Margaret
Spence.
p. cm. -- (World about us)
Includes index.
Summary: Examines the
different kinds of toxic waste,
ways in which they are disposed
of, and efforts to reduce the
amount produced.
ISBN 0-531-17297-X
1. Hazardous wastes--Juvenile
literature. [1. Hazardous
wastes--Environmental aspects.
2. Pollution.] I. Title. II. Series.
TD1030.5.S69    1992
363.72'87--dc20
91-30535    CIP   AC

Printed in Belgium

# Contents

# Introduction

There are many kinds of waste, from household garbage to industrial pollution. Waste that is particularly dangerous is called toxic waste. Toxic waste contains chemicals that are very poisonous to both humans and the environment. Until recently, toxic waste was either buried, dumped, or burned. However, as we become more aware of its dangers, new ways of disposing of toxic waste must be found.

# Toxic waste

Toxic waste is different from other types of waste because it contains substances that are always dangerous. Pesticides are used in farming to kill insects, and PCBs are used in the electrical industry. Both contain chemicals that can be harmful to the liver and kidneys if they get into the environment. They may even cause cancer. Some toxic chemicals are harmful even in tiny amounts, others are harmful only in large amounts.

Countries that have a lot of industry tend to produce the greatest amount of toxic waste.

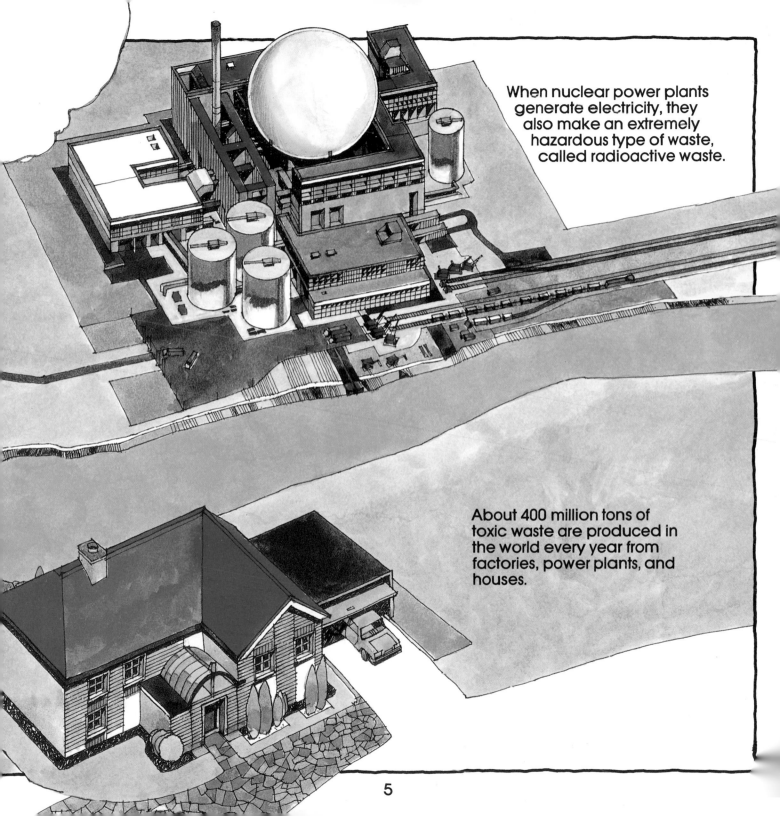

When nuclear power plants generate electricity, they also make an extremely hazardous type of waste, called radioactive waste.

About 400 million tons of toxic waste are produced in the world every year from factories, power plants, and houses.

# Industrial hazards

The largest amount of toxic waste is created by chemical industries. Factories often use poisonous chemicals when they make their products, and the wastes that are left over can be toxic. For example, when chlorine is used as a bleach in the paper industry, the waste produced contains dioxins which are extremely toxic substances. Dioxins can cause cancer if they enter the body in the food we eat or the air we breathe.

Wastes from industry are released into rivers, into the air, and dumped on the land.

Toxic waste often has to be transported on public roads or railroads. In the United States between 1980-85, there were 7,000 accidents involving trucks carrying toxic waste.

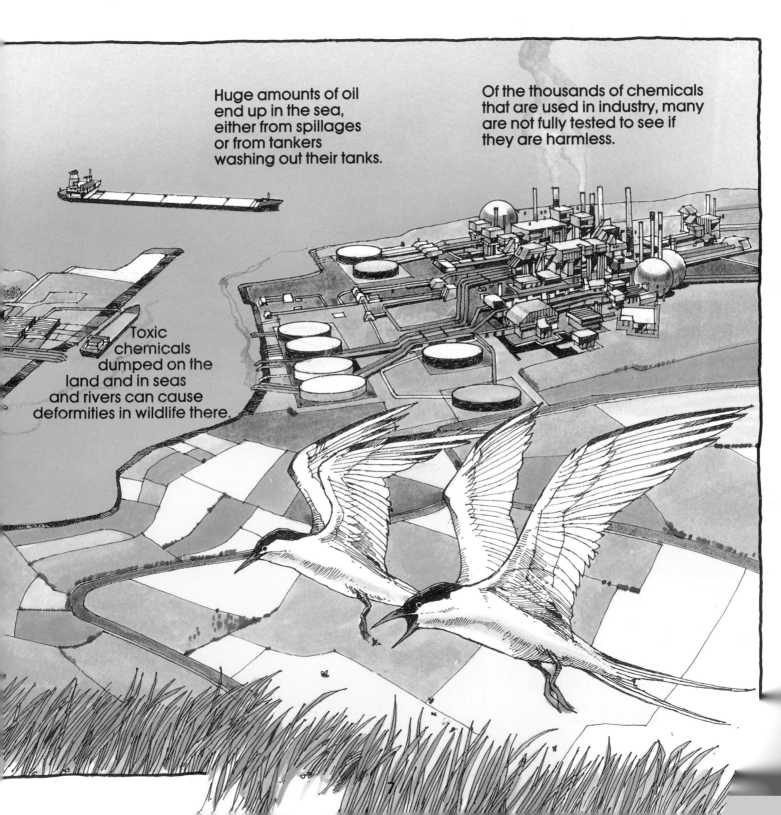

Huge amounts of oil end up in the sea, either from spillages or from tankers washing out their tanks.

Of the thousands of chemicals that are used in industry, many are not fully tested to see if they are harmless.

Toxic chemicals dumped on the land and in seas and rivers can cause deformities in wildlife there.

# In the ground

One of the most common ways to dispose of toxic waste is to bury or dump it in huge holes in the ground called landfill sites. Landfill sites are lined with thick layers of clay or tough plastic. When the holes have been filled, the area is covered and may be used as a park or golf course. But landfills do have drawbacks. Floods or heavy rains can wash the toxic wastes into the soil, poisoning the water supply below.

In the past, dangerous mixtures of chemicals were dumped with little thought to their effects on the environment. Many of the sites used now need urgent attention before they become harmful to people living nearby.

About 80% of the waste produced in the United States ends up in landfill sites. As the waste rots, it can produce explosive gases, like methane. These gases may be dangerous if they seep into nearby buildings.

8

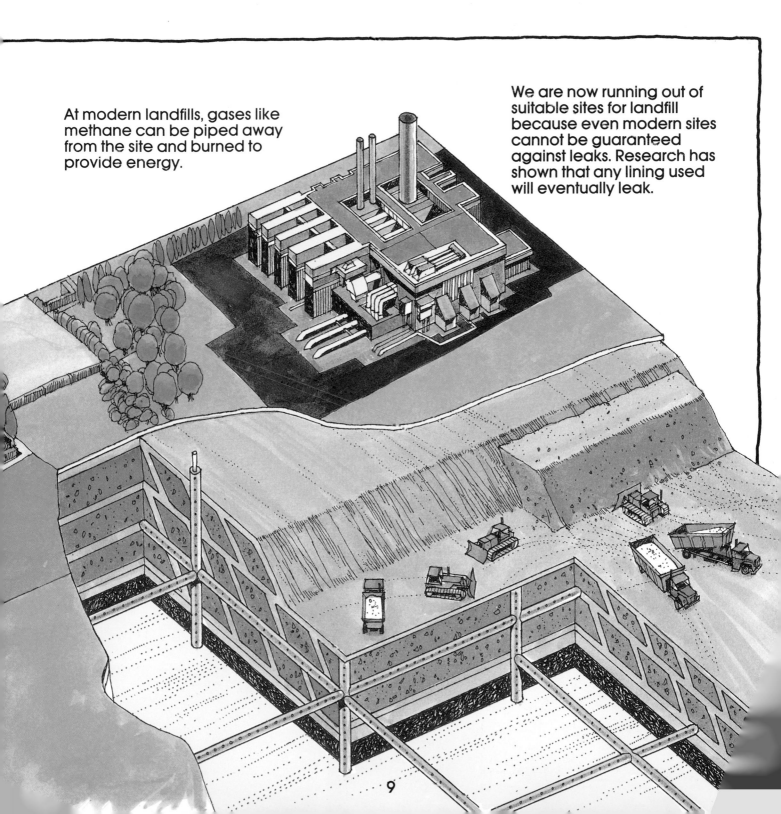

At modern landfills, gases like methane can be piped away from the site and burned to provide energy.

We are now running out of suitable sites for landfill because even modern sites cannot be guaranteed against leaks. Research has shown that any lining used will eventually leak.

# Dangerous dumps

In 1977, Love Canal in New York state brought the dangers of toxic waste to world attention. For over 20 years, an unfinished canal was used as a dumpsite for toxic waste. In 1953, the site was covered and houses and schools were built there. In 1976, flooding caused the buried chemicals to leak. The area had to be evacuated as people became ill. Over 80 different chemicals were found buried at the site.

A site near Louisville, Kentucky, was nicknamed the "Valley of the Drums" after 17,000 rotting barrels were dumped there. The contents of the barrels are unknown, but hazardous chemicals have been found leaking into streams leading to the nearby Ohio River.

New York Bight, off the coast of New Jersey, has been used as an ocean dumping ground for nearly 60 years. The seabed in the area is covered with a highly toxic black sludge which is poisonous to shellfish.

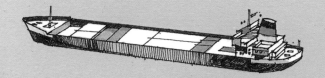

Industries on the banks of rivers, like the Rhine in Europe, often discharge untreated liquid waste directly into the water.

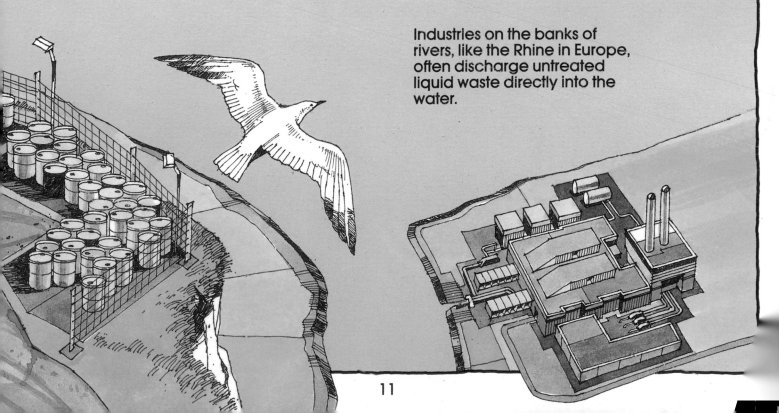

# Up in smoke

Burning toxic waste in a special device called an incinerator greatly reduces the amount of solid waste to be buried or dumped. Also, the heat produced by the burning waste can provide power for homes nearby. However, incineration costs three times as much as landfill and certain materials, like metals, cannot be destroyed by burning. Moreover, there is a danger that extremely poisonous gases, like dioxins, may escape into the air.

Burning toxic waste at sea is much cheaper because the gases produced are not treated to make them safe. But concern about the effects of these gases on life in the sea led to the banning of ocean incineration in 1991.

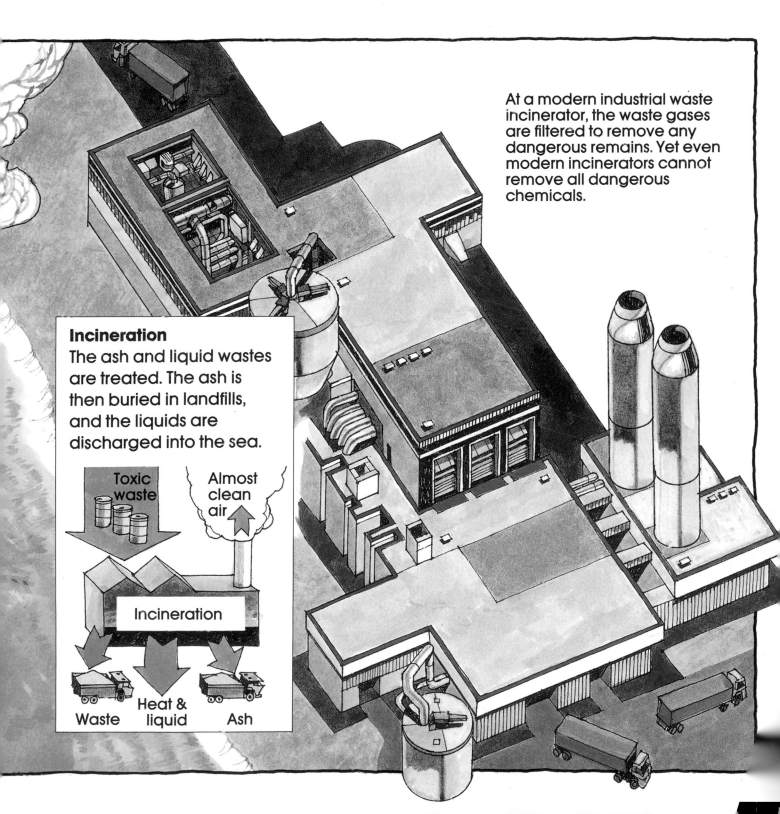

At a modern industrial waste incinerator, the waste gases are filtered to remove any dangerous remains. Yet even modern incinerators cannot remove all dangerous chemicals.

**Incineration**

The ash and liquid wastes are treated. The ash is then buried in landfills, and the liquids are discharged into the sea.

Toxic waste

Almost clean air

Incineration

Waste

Heat & liquid

Ash

# Toxic air pollution

When coal and oil are burned, sulfur dioxide gas is given off and mixes with the water in clouds. The rain that falls from these clouds contains very weak sulfuric acid and is called acid rain. Toxic gases are also given off in the exhaust fumes of cars and trucks. In sunlight, tiny particles of unburned gasoline, called hydrocarbons, mix with nitrogen oxides in the air to make ozone. Ozone is poisonous at ground level.

In some cities, the air pollution is so bad that people have to wear masks or stay indoors.

Cars and trucks also give off the metal lead in their exhaust fumes. High levels of lead in the air are harmful to pregnant women and may lead to brain damage in young children.

The effects of air pollution from factories, cars, and trucks trap heat close to the ground. This could lead to rising temperatures, or global warming.

# Domestic waste

Not all toxic waste is the result of industry. Every year, millions of tons of domestic waste, like paper or plastic packaging, old batteries from toys, clocks and radios, and even old TVs and refrigerators, are thrown away. Most of this waste ends up in landfills, where different chemicals can mix together to form toxic substances.

Used motor oil and bottles of pesticides from the garden are often poured down the drain. Both may end up polluting rivers or seas.

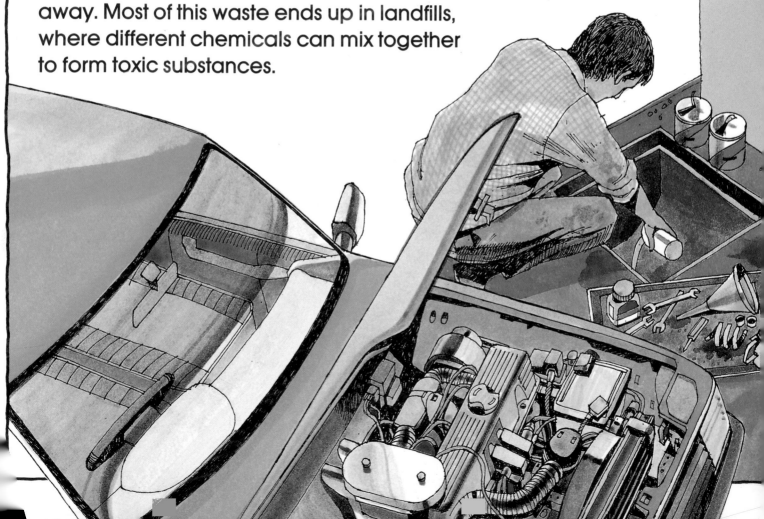

Furniture polish, bleach, cleaning solutions, and soaps are all used around the home and may be hazardous if not disposed of properly.

## Water works
In most developed countries, houses are connected to sewers by an underground pipe which carries the dirty water to a sewage plant to be treated.

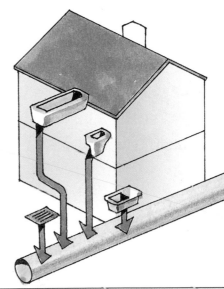

Solvents are substances that dissolve other substances. They include things like paint thinner and nail polish remover, which are thrown away with domestic waste, and are extremely toxic.

# Sewage

Although sewage is not often thought of as a toxic waste, it can be contaminated with poisonous chemicals which get into the sewage pipes from nearby factories or houses. For example, metals like lead or cobalt cannot be easily removed from sewage. The sludge that is produced when sewage is treated may contain traces of these metals. If the sludge is then used as a fertilizer, the metals can enter the soil, poisoning crops and the people or animals who eat them.

2. The sewage is treated to remove any germs and the solids are separated from the liquids.

1. The water and solids flow to a sewage treatment plant. Here, the sewage is filtered for large, bulky objects like diapers.

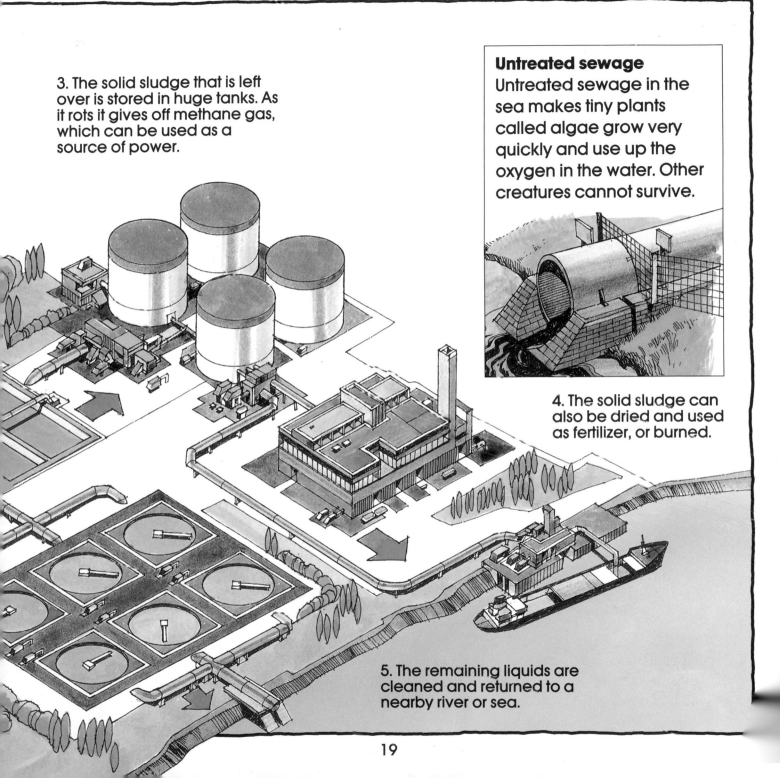

3. The solid sludge that is left over is stored in huge tanks. As it rots it gives off methane gas, which can be used as a source of power.

**Untreated sewage**
Untreated sewage in the sea makes tiny plants called algae grow very quickly and use up the oxygen in the water. Other creatures cannot survive.

4. The solid sludge can also be dried and used as fertilizer, or burned.

5. The remaining liquids are cleaned and returned to a nearby river or sea.

19

# Nuclear waste

Nuclear power plants create electricity by splitting tiny particles, called atoms. The waste that is produced is radioactive. Even in tiny amounts, radioactivity can be harmful. Nuclear waste is perhaps the most dangerous of all types of waste, because it cannot be destroyed and remains hazardous for thousands of years. Low- and intermediate-level waste contain less radioactivity than high-level waste, which is extremely dangerous.

When nuclear weapons are taken apart, the pieces are contaminated with high levels of radioactivity.

**Radioactive mines**
Uranium is used in nuclear power plants. It is found in rock along with a gas called radon which is radioactive. When the rock is crushed to extract uranium, poisonous radon gas is also released.

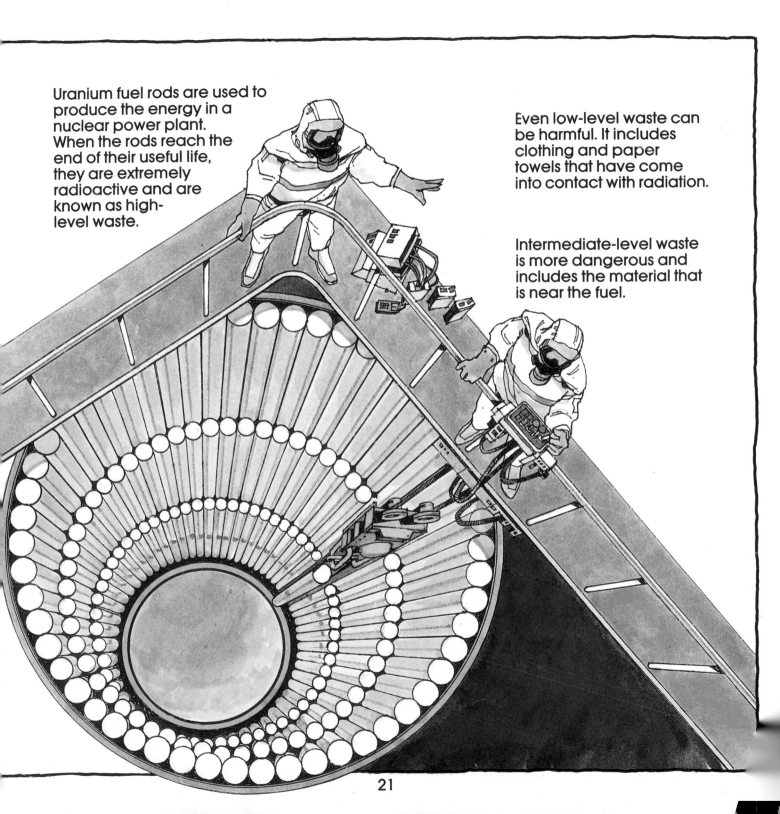

Uranium fuel rods are used to produce the energy in a nuclear power plant. When the rods reach the end of their useful life, they are extremely radioactive and are known as high-level waste.

Even low-level waste can be harmful. It includes clothing and paper towels that have come into contact with radiation.

Intermediate-level waste is more dangerous and includes the material that is near the fuel.

# Storing nuclear waste

Nuclear waste must be carefully stored to stop radiation from escaping. Low- and intermediate-level wastes are covered in steel and concrete and stored under-ground. High-level waste is more difficult to store completely safely. Usually it is covered in steel or concrete and kept cool in huge tanks of water. It can also be mixed with liquid glass, poured into steel containers and buried. This process is called vitrification.

Some countries have built special concrete sites in which to store the low- and intermediate-level wastes that come not only from power plants, but also from hospitals and industry.

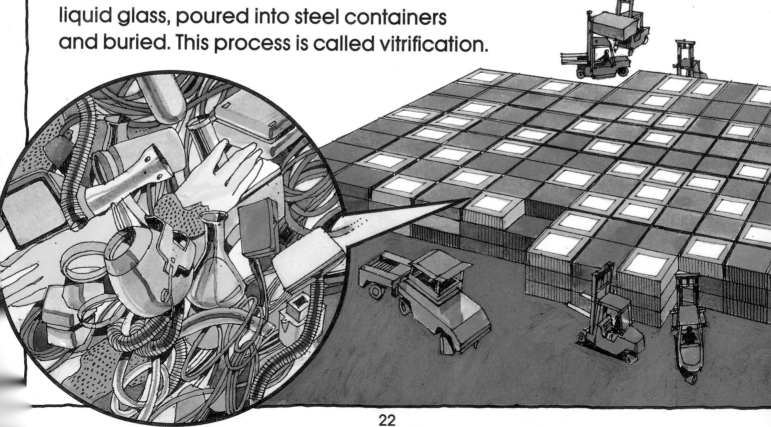

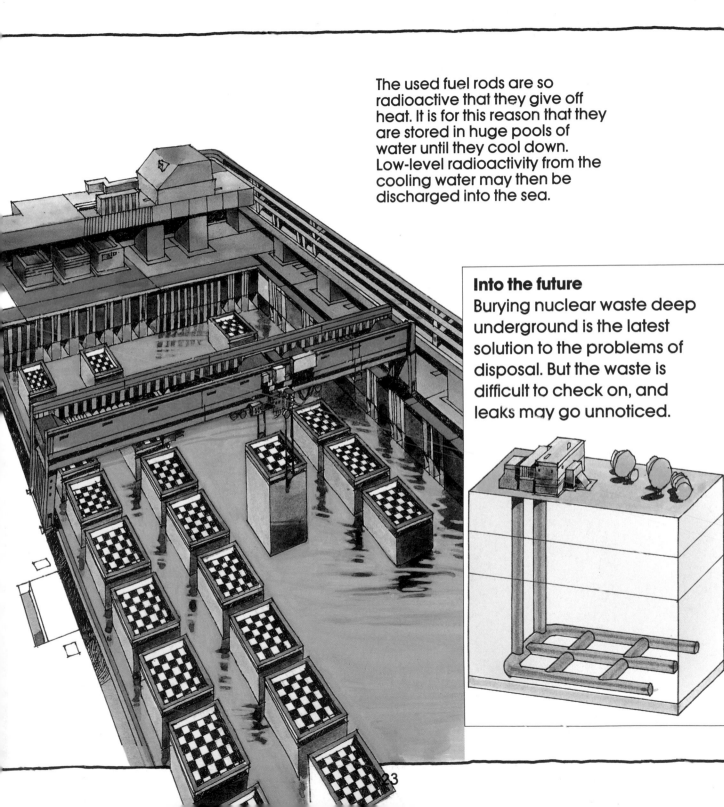

The used fuel rods are so radioactive that they give off heat. It is for this reason that they are stored in huge pools of water until they cool down. Low-level radioactivity from the cooling water may then be discharged into the sea.

### Into the future
Burying nuclear waste deep underground is the latest solution to the problems of disposal. But the waste is difficult to check on, and leaks may go unnoticed.

# Toxic waste trade

As controls on the disposal of toxic waste become stricter in rich countries, shipments of waste to poorer countries, where there are no such controls, are increasing. Poorer countries often accept dangerous waste in return for money. However, often these countries cannot deal with the waste safely, so it becomes an even bigger threat to the environment and the people there.

In 1988, an Italian company illegally dumped toxic waste in Nigeria. The waste was removed on a ship called the *Karin B.*, which then toured Europe for months looking for a dumpsite, before being forced to return to Italy.

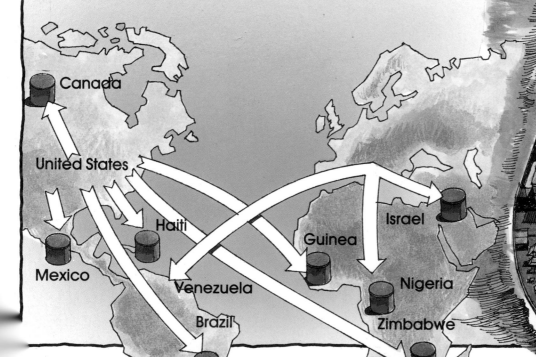

Canada

United States

Haiti

Mexico

Venezuela

Brazil

Guinea

Israel

Nigeria

Zimbabwe

Poorer countries are often promised aid, in the form of food or farming equipment, if they accept dangerous wastes.

The lack of regulations in poorer countries has often led to illegal and dangerous dumping. Toxic wastes have been poured along roadsides, or stored in unmarked barrels which may rot and leak.

# Taking action

The dangers of toxic waste can no longer be ignored. People should be encouraged to buy more goods made from natural materials, which are safer to make and dispose of. Stricter laws controlling toxic waste have already been introduced in Denmark, Sweden, and the United States, and clean production is encouraged there where possible. This means that resources are used efficiently, and the amount of waste is reduced.

In 1978, a fire broke out at a waste dump in the United States. Residents in the area suffered lung, skin, and eye damage from the chemical fumes and the area had to be evacuated.

In 1986, a chemical spill into the River Rhine killed all life in the river for 60 miles. In some countries, industries are encouraged to use substances that are not based on toxic chemicals.

In 1974 at Flixborough, England, 28 people died when a container of toxic chemicals exploded. Using less hazardous chemicals in industry would prevent such accidents.

# Did you know?

In the past it was thought that dioxins could move through soil very quickly, contaminating a large area in a short space of time. But recent research has shown that dioxins seem to move less than an inch every 400-5,000 years, which could make cleaning up affected areas much easier in the future.

TBT (tributyltin oxide) is painted on the bottom of ships to keep them free from barnacles and weeds. It also contains the metal tin and is extremely toxic. As the tin dissolves into the sea, it has serious effects on shellfish there. Oysters in affected areas are much smaller than usual, and sea snails are unable to breed.

On Johnston Island in the Pacific Ocean, an incinerator has been built to get rid of the piles of chemical weapons that are too old to be used, but could be dangerous if left on dumps. The weapons contain very poisonous chemicals. There are fears that toxic gases could escape if these chemicals are burned.

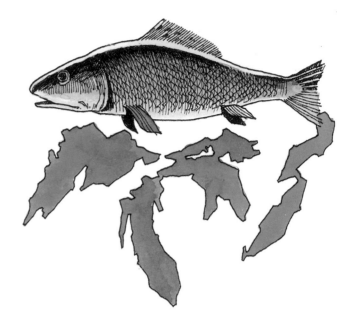

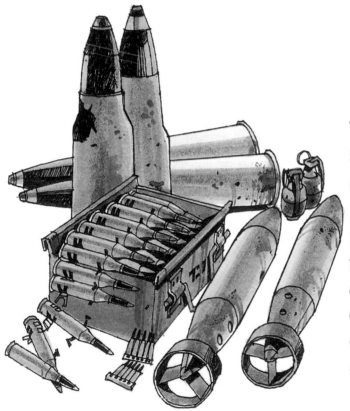

The Great Lakes in the United States and Canada provide drinking water for over 24 million people. But the lakes are heavily polluted with toxic chemicals from nearby industry. The drinking water drawn from Lake Ontario for the city of Toronto, Canada, was found to contain over 50 harmful chemicals.

In many parts of the world, the air is severely polluted by toxic chemicals from industry and transportation. In Mexico City, the air is as harmful as smoking 40 cigarettes a day. And in Cubato, Brazil, air pollution is so bad the trees there are black stumps, and birds or insects cannot survive.

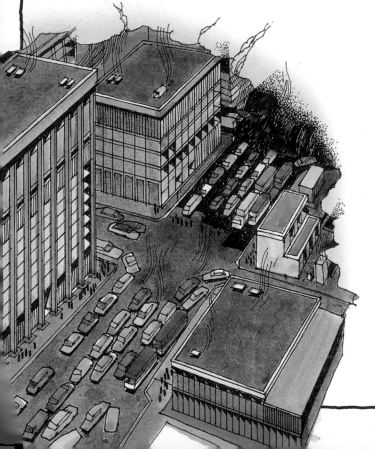

Toxic chemicals like PCBs (polychlorinated biphenyls) remain in the environment for a very long time. The use of PCBs has been banned in many countries, but they can still leak from old equipment. Traces of PCBs have even been found in Arctic snow, hundreds of miles from the nearest factory.

# Glossary

**Atoms**
The tiny particles of which everything is made. Atoms are made of even tinier particles, called protons, neutrons, and electrons.

**Dioxins**
Substances which can be extremely harmful if people come into contact with them. There are at least 75 different types of dioxins.

**Fertilizers**
Chemicals that farmers put on crops to make them grow.

**Global warming**
The gases which trap heat close to the earth's surface are called greenhouse gases. When too many of these gases are produced, the temperatures on earth go up. This is known as global warming.

**PCBs (Polychlorinated biphenyls)**
Toxic chemicals used in the electrical industry. PCBs stay in the environment for a very long time, and can cause terrible deformities in birds and other animals.

**Radioactivity**
Produced when a radioactive atom breaks down, or decays. Radioactivity can be harmful to living things. Radioactive waste comes from nuclear power plants and from medical uses. It can be dangerous for thousands of years.

# Index

**A**
air pollution 6, 12, 14, 15, 29
ash 13

**B**
burning 3, 12, 13
burying 3, 8

**C**
cancer 4, 6

**D**
dioxins 6, 12, 30, 31
disposal 3, 8, 10, 22, 24, 25
domestic waste 3, 16-18
dumping 3, 8, 10, 11

**F**
fertilizer 18, 31

**I**
incinerators 12, 13, 29
industry 4, 6, 7, 11, 27

**L**
landfill sites 8-12, 16
Love Canal 10

**M**
methane 8, 9, 19

**N**
nuclear waste 5, 20-23

**O**
oil 7, 14, 16

**P**
PCBs 4, 30, 31
pesticides 4, 16

**S**
sewage 18, 19

**T**
TBT 28
transportation 6